The Old Boot

Chris Baines
& Penny Ives

Crocodile Books, USA

An imprint of Interlink Publishing Group, Inc.
NEW YORK

When it's dark, and we're fast asleep
in bed, all kinds of little creatures
are hard at work outside, searching
for food down in the long grass.
Some of them have lots and lots of
legs. They can move very quickly.
Some of them have no legs at all.
They slither along very slowly.
All these creatures of the night need
to find a safe, dark place to hide
before the sun comes up.

Someone has thrown away
an old boot. It has been lying in
the grass for a long time, and the
creatures of the night use it as their
home. Each one has its own special place
under the boot. The worms have a hole each,
deep in the earth. The big squidgy slug has a slug-shaped
space, the long thin creature with lots and lots of legs has
its own long thin space. The woodlice like to keep
close together.
Can you see where they're all hiding?

When the creatures of the night come home to their old boot after a hard night hunting for food, the ants are just about to start work. Ants sleep at night, like us, and love to work all day in the warm, bright sunshine. They have a nest under the toe of the old boot, with lots of winding tunnels down in the earth. Their first job each morning is to carry the baby ants up out of the cool, damp tunnels, and lay them out like big white blobs on the ground under the boot. It's warmer here, and the blobs are still safe — hidden from birds and other creatures that might eat them.

The ants go off hunting for food in the long grass, and
bring back all kinds of things to their nest.
Sometimes the ants bring things they can't eat.
Big shiny seeds are much too hard, so they get dumped
among the sleeping creatures of the night, in the
dark, damp space underneath the boot.

One sunny afternoon, the night
creatures are all asleep, the
baby ant blobs are warming on
the earth above the nest, and
the ants are hunting for things
to eat. Suddenly the earth begins
to shake. A foot crashes down
beside the boot, and then —

the old boot is lifted high into the air and a loud voice shouts, "Ugh! It's full of creepy-crawlies!" The old boot drops to the ground again.

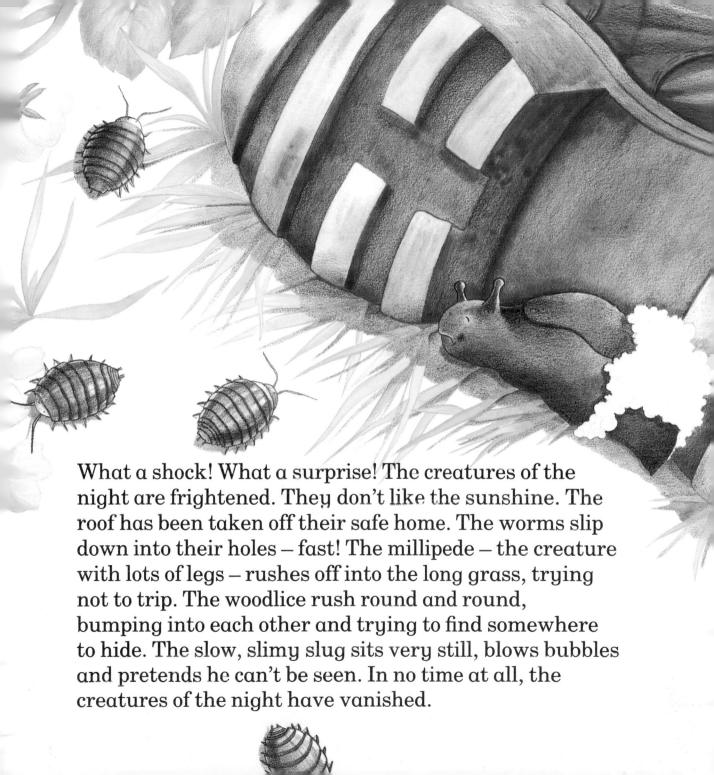

What a shock! What a surprise! The creatures of the
night are frightened. They don't like the sunshine. The
roof has been taken off their safe home. The worms slip
down into their holes – fast! The millipede – the creature
with lots of legs – rushes off into the long grass, trying
not to trip. The woodlice rush round and round,
bumping into each other and trying to find somewhere
to hide. The slow, slimy slug sits very still, blows bubbles
and pretends he can't be seen. In no time at all, the
creatures of the night have vanished.

All that crashing and banging brings the ants rushing to save their baby ant blobs. Now that the boot has gone, the white blobs are very easy to see. The ants pull and push, push and pull, and they take the baby ant blobs down into the nest. But they're too late to save all of them. A hungry bird swoops down and pecks up one or two.

Not everything is unhappy to be uncovered. Now the boot has been moved, the big hard seed is watered by the rain, and the bright sunshine makes it burst open and start to grow. In just a few days, a little green plant is growing happily in the bare earth where the boot once stood. And what about the creatures of the night, and the ants, and the baby ant blobs?
Where do you think they are?

Back under their dear old boot!
The ants have dug a new nest. The worms
have a brand new hole each. The slug and
the millipede both have a space that's just
the right shape — and the woodlice have
found a bigger, darker, safer hole than
they ever dreamed of before.
Can you see where they're
all hiding?